GOOGLE PIXEL WATCH GUIDE 2022

Step by step guide to get the most of your pixel watch

Obed Peterson

Contents

Introduction

The Google Pixel Watch is a relatively simple and uncluttered smartwatch that follows in the footsteps of the design aesthetic of Google's other Pixel smartphones. It is only available in one size, which is 41mm, and its overall shape is rounded. It has a digital crown that appears to be somewhat comparable to the digital crown that is included on the Apple Watch. However, it does not sit quite as flush with the curved chassis. There are several grooves on the crown button that you can feel. This may make it more enjoyable to use the smartwatch.

In addition, the right-hand side of the Pixel Watch features a single navigation button that is positioned directly above the digital crown. On the other hand, the cutouts for the microphone and speaker are located on the left side.

In conjunction with the debut of the Pixel Watch, Google is also releasing a selection of interchangeable straps. There are a total of seven different band types, and each one comes in a variety of colors. However, they are only compatible with the Pixel Watch. Google made a comparison between switching out the bands on the Pixel Watch and switching out the lenses on a camera.

This guide will provide you with all of the information you require on the Google Pixel Watch, including how to make the most of its features.

Chapter 1: Accessibility features on Google Pixel Watch

Customize the Google Pixel Watch with accessibility settings such as magnification and font size. Triple-tapping the button next to the crown enables the TalkBack text-to-speech accessibility shortcut during setup.

Enable accessibility features

On the Google Pixel Watch

1. Tap Settings on the Google Pixel Watch, followed by Accessibility.
2. Here, you may modify the magnification and other options.
3. Swipe down to adjust the font size, volume, and other settings.

On the Google Pixel watch application

1. On your mobile device, launch the Google Pixel Watch app.
2. To make tweaks, swipe down on the home screen and then tap Accessibility.

Audio feedback

Google Pixel Watch provides audio feedback for the time and notifications, along with options for how to respond. Use Audio Feedback with voice actions to send and respond to text messages on your watch, as well as make and receive phone calls. Gain a deeper understanding of Audio feedback.

Navigate your watch with wrist movements.

You can control your watch with wrist movements.

1. Swipe down on the Google Pixel Watch to access the Home Screen.
2. Tap Settings, followed by Gestures.
3. Turn on or off wrist gesture options.

Note that certain movements, such as Tilt-to-wake, decrease battery life.

Chapter 2: Set up Google Pixel Watch

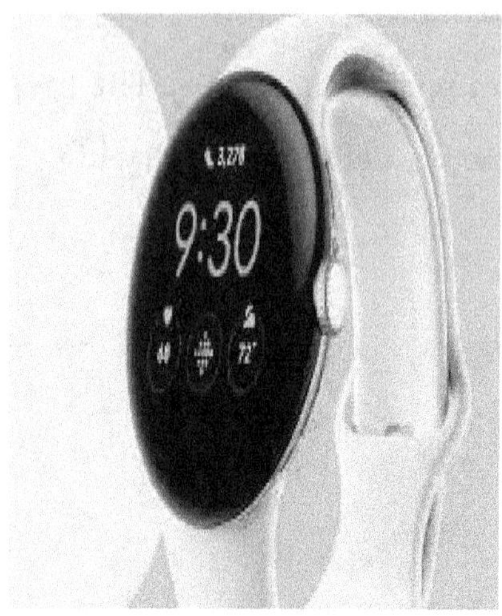

What you need to get started

- A google account
- Google Pixel Watch
- USB-C Magnetic Charging Cable (included with Google Pixel Watch)
- USB Type-C Adapter (not included)
- Android phone updated to version 8.0 or higher connected to either Wi-Fi or LTE

- For Google Pixel Watch LTE, you will be prompted to activate LTE service during setup.
- The latest version of the google pixel app.
  - Note: If you are in a supported nation and using a supported carrier, but you cannot locate the Google Pixel Watch app, check your Google Play Store account to ensure that the address on file is in a supported country or area.

- o Download and log into the Fitbit app for the optimal experience. Sign in with your existing Fitbit account or establish a new one.
- o Child Fitbit accounts are not supported.

Before you begin

- Charge your watch and phone fully.
- Turn on Bluetooth and Location settings on your phone.
- Attach the band of your choice to the watch and adjust the band and sizing to your liking.

Configure a Google Pixel Watch

1. Press the crown for three seconds to activate Google Pixel Watch.

2. Place your watch close to a Bluetooth-enabled Android 8.0+ smartphone. The display should suggest pairing may commence.

- Ensure you have the most recent version of the Google Pixel Watch app installed if you do not receive a pairing notification.

a. Enable Nearby sharing.

b. To link a new watch, open the app and follow the instructions provided.

c. Tap Google, then Devices & sharing, then Devices, and then Saved devices in your phone's Settings. If your Google Pixel Watch has been successfully linked, it will be displayed below.

3. Select your language and agree to the terms of service by following the on-screen prompts on your watch.

Note: You can activate the TalkBack text-to-speech accessibility shortcut during setup by triple-tapping the side button adjacent to the crown.

4. Follow the app's on-screen instructions and then pick Google Pixel Watch to begin pairing.

5. On both the app and the watch, a matching pairing code will be presented.

- If the codes are equal: On your phone, tap Pair. This could take many minutes.

- If the codes do not correspond: Reset your timepiece and try again. If the codes do not match, try these Android troubleshooting procedures.

6. Create a Google Account or sign in with an existing Google Account to proceed with the setup.

7. Additional on-screen questions can assist with configuration or connection:

- LTE
- Google Pay
- Google Assistant
- An individual lock screen PIN or pattern
- Other Google Play Store applications compatible with the Google Pixel Watch

8. Follow the remaining instructions on-screen.

9. Swipe down on the Google Pixel Watch and then tap Settings ⚙.

10. Select System followed by System updates.

Google Pixel Watch will perform an update check.

When your device and watch properly connect, the Google Pixel Watch app will display "Connected." When they do not, "Disconnected" will appear on the watch's display.

Set up Fitbit

1. To use the Google Pixel Watch, press the crown.

2. Tap Fitbit Today followed by Log In.

3. On your mobile device, log in. If you don't already have the Fitbit app on your phone, touch Install and then tap Install again. Initiate and then Join Fitbit. Then, follow the steps displayed on-screen to create a Fitbit account.

4. First-time Fitbit users: Select the Google Pixel Watch from the selection of watches during Fitbit account creation.

Current Fitbit users: Add Google Pixel Watch to your Fitbit profile by navigating to your account profile in the upper-left corner of the Fitbit app's home page, and then selecting "Add Device." Configure a Device.

5. When prompted, configure the app's permissions.

Set up LTE

If you have a Google Pixel Watch LTE, you will have a direct connection to your carrier and share a number with your phone, allowing notifications and messages to be synchronized. You can leave your phone at home and still utilize all accessible services.

1. Swipe down on the Google Pixel Watch and then tap Settings ⚙.
2. Select Connectivity followed by Mobile.
3. Verify that the status has been set to On.
4. On your mobile device, launch the Google Pixel Watch app.
5. Mobile network access then Create a new account.
6. Select Create a new profile with your mobile carrier.
7. Follow the on-screen prompts to log in to your network provider's account and finish setup.

Resolve problems with LTE activation

If you have previously acquired a device with an inactive e-SIM profile that was never erased, you may encounter difficulties activating LTE.

1. Charge and activate the Google Pixel Watch.
2. Swipe down on the Google Pixel Watch

and then tap Settings ⚙.

3. Tap Connectivity, followed by Mobile, and finally SIM status.

4. If there is an existing eSIM profile, reset eSIM by selecting Settings > Connectivity > Mobile > Advanced > Reset eSIM from the menu. Depending on the provider, you may be required to call to reactivate the eSIM.

Personalize watch face

Choose the watch face complexities that display the information that is most vital to you, such as your step count or the weather. Complications are watch face features that do more than display the time.

1. To personalize your existing watch face, press and maintain your finger on the face.

2. To customize the color, layout, and complexity, select Edit ✐.

3. Swipe left to navigate between the styles and complexity layouts.

i. Tap and hold your watch face to add a fresh face.

ii. Swipe to the left and press Add ✛.

iii. Select the desired watch face from the selection.

iv.   Swipe left to select the desired color, layout, and complexity.

If you choose the Photos watch face, you can add up to 30 images from your personal photo album.

Add tiles

You can add tiles for quickly accessible information and shortcuts to your most often performed operations.

1. Swipe to any tile on the Google Pixel Watch and press and hold the tile.

2. Tap Add ┼ .

3. Swipe up to navigate the tiles, then tap the one you wish to add.

Fix problems with set up

Charge the battery and enable Bluetooth as the first step.

1. View the Setup Pixel Watch video to validate that all steps have been performed correctly.

2. Confirm that the battery of the Google Pixel Watch is fully charged.

3. Ensure Bluetooth is enabled on your device.

Step 2: Resolve setup issues with the Google Pixel Watch

1. Confirm your proximity to the device. For Fast Pair to

function, your phone must be within 0.5 m (1.6 ft) of your Google Pixel Watch.

2. Ensure that both Bluetooth and Location are enabled on your phone.

3. Verify that your phone is linked to a Wi-Fi or cellular network.

Chapter 3: Play and download music on Google Pixel Watch

On Google Pixel Watch, you can listen to music via apps like YouTube Music1 and Spotify. Additional music apps are available in the Google Play store for Google Pixel Watch.

Google Assistant allows you to adjust the volume and the currently playing track.

- Google Pixel Watch LTE: Stream music without the need to download or have your phone handy.
- Google Pixel Watch Wi-Fi: When your phone is nearby or you're connected to Wi-Fi, you can download and store songs on your watch or stream music.

Youtube Music requirements

- Google account Internet access (streaming)
- Start your YouTube Premium Music trial

Start your Youtube Music Premium trial

The Google Pixel Watch includes a three-month trial of YouTube Music Premium.

1. Tap the button next to the crown on your Google Pixel Watch.
2. Swipe up and select All apps, followed by YouTube Music, and finally Open on phone .
3. Follow the on-screen steps in the Google Pixel Watch app to sign into or create your YouTube account and activate your trial.

Smart Downloads on Youtube Music

Set up automatic downloads of recommended music based on your listening history to discover new music.

1. On your mobile device, launch Google Pixel Watch .
2. Sign in to your music YouTube account.
3. Tap the crown on your Pixel Watch.
4. Tap and swipe up YouTube Music.
5. Swipe up and select Settings, followed by Downloads.
6. Choose the quantity of songs you wish to update and download on a regular basis.

This will be updated every night when your battery has more over 40 percent charge and you are connected to Wi-

Fi or LTE. Depending on your download settings, it can also update over unlimited mobile data.

7. You can play, pause, or delete music to enhance your recommendations, and you can select the music to download.

8. Reconnect to the internet every thirty days to preserve downloaded music.

Chapter 4: Google Pixel Watch Technical & Device Specifications

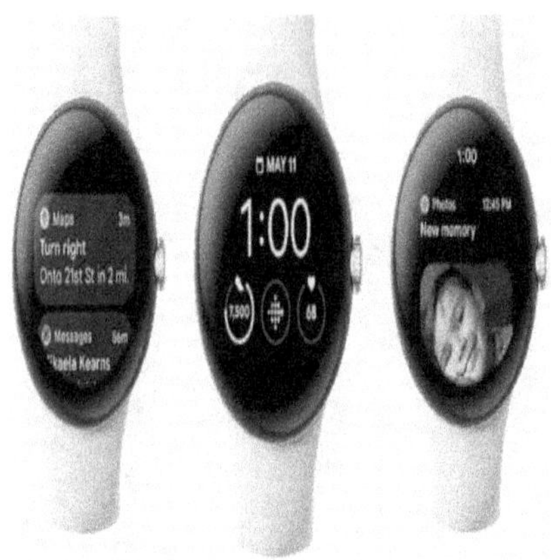

Google Pixel Watch Specifications

Colors[1]

Matte Black Stainless Steel case / Obsidian Active band

Polished Silver Stainless Steel case / Charcoal Active band

Polished Silver Stainless Steel case / Chalk Active band

Champagne Gold Stainless Steel case / Hazel Active band

Materials and finishes

Case: 80% recycled stainless steel

Active band: Fluoroelastomer with soft-touch coating

Dimensions and Weight

Diameter: 41 mm

Height: 12.3 mm

Weight: 36 g (without band)

Connectivity

4G LTE and UMTS[2]

Bluetooth® 5.0

Wi-Fi 802.11 b/g/n 2.4GHz

NFC

FeliCa

GPS

GPS

GLONASS

BeiDou

Galileo

Compatibility

Android 8.0 or newer[3]

Display

Custom 3D Corning® Gorilla®
Glass

320 ppi AMOLED display
with DCI-P3 color

Brightness boost up to 1000
nits

Always-on display

Band Size

Active band: Small and large
band sizes included

- Small fits wrists 130-
  175 mm around

- Large fits wrists 165-
  210 mm around

**Power (Battery and
Charging)**

294 mAh (typical)

Built-in rechargeable
lithium-ion battery

Up to 24 hours[4]

USB-C® magnetic charging
cable

100% charge in 2.5 hours[4]

Chip

Exynos 9110 SoC

Cortex M33 co-processor

OS

Wear OS 3.5

Storage and Memory

32 GB eMMC FLASH[5]

2 GB SDRAM

Sensors

Compass

Altimeter

Blood oxygen sensor[6]

Multipurpose electrical sensor

Optical heart rate sensor[7]

Accelerometer

Gyroscope

Ambient light sensor

Interaction

Side button

Haptic crown

Premium haptics

Audio

Built-in microphone

Built-in speaker

Features

Fitbit health and fitness

Always-on display

Google Maps

Google Wallet[8]

Google Assistant

Messages and notifications

YouTube Music

FeliCa

NFC

Emergency SOS[9]

International emergency calling[9]

Fall detection (up to 32 g-forces)[10] (Coming soon)

Interchangeable band design

Durability and Water Resistance

Custom 3D Corning® Gorilla® Glass 5

5 ATM[11]

What's in the Box

Google Pixel Watch

Active band (small and large wristbands)

USB-C® magnetic charging cable

Quick Start Guide

Google Pixel Watch Accessory Charger Specifications

Compatibility

Compatible with Google Pixel Watch

Wattage

5W

Requires a USB-C® PD compatible adapter (not included)

Dimensions

Magnetic charger diameter: 33 mm

Cable length: 1 meter

Connectors

Magnetic charger to USB-C

Color

Snow

Material

Charger: made with 50% recycled plastic[12]

USB-C® cable: TPE

What's in the Box

Google Pixel Watch USB-C® magnetic charging cable (1 m)

Power adapter not included

Weight

28 g

Google Pixel Watch Accessory Band Tech Specifications

Active Band

Compatibility

Compatible with Google Pixel Watch

Materials

Band: Flouroelastomer with soft-touch coating

Clasp and lugs: Stainless steel

Colors[1]

Obsidian

Charcoal

Chalk

Lemongrass

Hazel

Sizing

Small and large band sizes included

Small: Fits wrists 130-175 mm around

Large: Fits wrists 165-210 mm around

Woven band

Compatibility

Compatible with Google Pixel Watch

Materials

Band: Recycled PET yarn

Clasp and lugs: 50% post-consumer recycled content plastic, stainless steel[13]

Sweat & Water Resistance

Sweat and water resistant

Colors[1]

Coral

Lemongrass

Ivy

Sizing

One size: Fits wrists 137-203 mm around

Stretch band

Compatibility

Compatible with Google Pixel Watch

Materials

Band: Recycled polyester and spandex yarns[14]

Lugs: 50% post-consumer recycled content plastic

Sweat & Water Resistance

Sweat resistant

Colors[1]

Linen

Rose

Obsidian

Sizing

Extra Small: Fits wrists 130-150 mm around

Small: Fits wrists 140-160 mm around

Medium: Fits wrists 155-175 mm around

Large: Fits wrists 170-200 mm around

Extra Large: Fits wrists 190–210 mm around

Metal Mesh band (Coming soon)

Compatibility

Compatible with Google Pixel Watch

Materials

Band and lugs: Stainless steel

Clasp: Magnet + stainless steel

Sweat & Water Resistance

Not sweat or water resistant

Colors[1]

Polished Silver

Champagne Gold

Matte Black

Sizing

One size: Fits wrists 137-203 mm around

Classic Metal Links band (Coming soon)

Compatibility

Compatible with Google Pixel Watch

Materials

Stainless steel

Sweat & Water Resistance

Not sweat or water resistant

Colors[1]

Brushed Silver

Matte Black

Sizing

One size: Fits wrists 137-203 mm around

Two-Tone Leather band

Compatibility

Compatible with Google Pixel Watch

Materials

Band: Italian leather

Clasp and lugs: Stainless steel

Colors[1]

Linen

Chalk

Charcoal

Sweat & Water Resistance

Not sweat or water resistant

Sizing

Small: Fits wrists 137-170 mm around

Large: Fits wrists 171-203 mm around

Crafted Leather band

Compatibility

Compatible with Google Pixel Watch

Materials

Band: Italian leather

Clasp and lugs: Stainless steel

Sweat & Water Resistance

Not sweat or water resistant

Colors[1]

Ivy

Obsidian

Sizing

Small: Fits wrists 137-170 mm around

Large: Fits wrists 171-203 mm around

Chapter 5:

Emergency SOS and fall detection on Google Pixel Watch

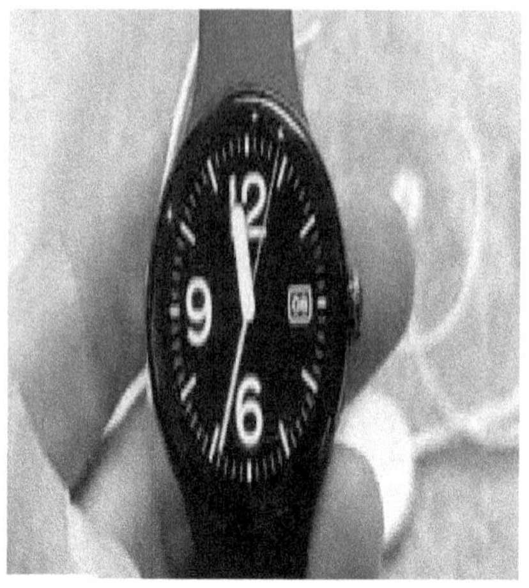

If you require assistance, your Google Pixel Watch can link you to emergency services. If you've unlocked your watch at least once since its initialization, you can call an emergency contact without unlocking it1.

To contact emergency services, the Google Pixel Watch Wi-Fi must be within range of your phone and connected through Bluetooth. If your watch is not connected to a phone, you will be unable to make a call.

Google Pixel Watch LTE requires an active LTE connection in order to contact emergency services when your phone is not nearby.

Set up Emergency SOS

Emergency SOS is a quick way to call for help in an emergency by pressing the crown five times in rapid succession. You can choose another receiver, including an emergency contact, instead of calling emergency services by default.

Note: This does not activate the Emergency SOS feature on your Pixel phone.

On Google Pixel Watch

1. Swipe down on the Google Pixel Watch and then tap Settings  .

2. Select Safety & Emergency, followed by Emergency SOS.

3. Activate features such as the emergency gesture, alarm, and primary contact selection.

On the Google Pixel Watch application

1. On your mobile device, launch the Google Pixel Watch app. Google Pixel Watch

2. Select Watch preferences, followed by Safety and Emergency, then Emergency SOS.

3. Turn on "Safety features."

Add emergency phone numbers

Add numerous emergency contacts and designate one as the primary contact.

1. Swipe down on the Google Pixel Watch and then tap Settings  .

2. Select Safety & Emergency, followed by Emergency SOS.

3. Select Add contact. Choose to enable or refuse access to your

phone's stored
contacts.

4. Tap the contact's
   name, followed by
   their phone number.

5. Tap Emergency
   Services or a contact
   from the list of added
   emergency contacts to
   select a primary
   emergency contact.
   Now, their card will be
   highlighted.

You can also add emergency
contacts to your Pixel's
Personal safety app.

Remove emergency contacts

1. Swipe down on the
   Google Pixel Watch
   and then tap Settings

   .

2. Select Safety &
   Emergency, followed
   by Emergency SOS.

3. Tap Edit contacts.

4. Tap Delete next to the
   contact you wish to
   delete.

Use Emergency SOS

To contact emergency
services from your Google
Pixel Watch, press the crown
five times. A conventional
call to emergency services is
placed, and you can
communicate with
emergency responders as
usual. If Emergency Location
Service is enabled on your
Google Pixel Watch and the
emergency responders in
your area are equipped with
ELS, they may also receive
your location.

It is possible that the Google
Pixel Watch Wi-Fi cannot
dial all emergency numbers
in all countries.

Disable Emergency SOS

1. To use the Google
   Pixel Watch, press the
   crown.
2. Touch Personal Safety
   and then Emergency
   SOS by scrolling
   down.
3. Turn off the
   Emergency gesture.

Accidental calls

Do not hang up if you
accidentally dial Emergency
SOS and emergency services
are contacted. Inform the
operator that the call was
made in error and that you
do not require assistance.

Fall detection

Google Pixel Watch will
include fall detection starting
this Winter (Summer in
Australia). When a heavy fall
is detected, your Google Pixel
Watch will inform you and
ask whether you want to dial
911.

Note that neither Australia
nor Germany support
automatic dialing of
emergency numbers.

Chapter 6: Change settings, alarms, and notifications on Google Pixel Watch

Customize watch face

Choose the watch face complexities that display the information that is most vital to you, such as your step count or the weather. Complications are watch face features that do more than display the time.

To personalize your existing watch face:

1. Press and hold the face of your watch.
2. To customize the color, layout, and complexity, select Edit ✎ .
3. Swipe left to navigate between the styles and complexity layouts.

To add a new watch face:

1. Press and hold the face of your watch.
2. Swipe to the left and press Add + .
3. Select the desired watch face from the selection.
4. Swipe left to select the desired color, layout, and complexity.

If you choose the Photos watch face, you can add up to 30 images from your personal photo album.

Add tiles

You can add tiles to provide quick access to frequently used information and activities.

1. Swipe to any tile on the Google Pixel Watch and tap and hold the tile.

2. Tap Add ✛ .

3. Swipe up to navigate the tiles, then touch the one you wish to add.

Adjust display, brightness, and audio settings

To alter further Pixel Watch settings:

1. Touch the watch face to illuminate the display.

2. Drag down from the top of the display.

3. Tap Settings ⚙ .

From here, one may:

- Lock your watch's display

- Adjust audio settings

Configure and administer alarms and notifications

On Google Pixel Watch, you can receive notifications for both your watch and your phone's apps.

To configure which apps receive notifications:

1. On your mobile device, launch the

Google Pixel Watch
app .

2. Tap Notifications
under "Settings."

3. Choose watch or
phone apps and toggle
notifications on or off
for each.

Set notification modes

You can select several
settings based on your
preferences for individual
apps and watch
functionalities. Swipe down
from the top of the screen on
the Google Pixel Watch and
tap an icon to rapidly switch
between:

- **Airplane mode**:
Turn off all radios on
your watch, including
Bluetooth, Wi-Fi, LTE,
and GPS/GNSS. Each

of these can be turned
on independently.

- **Theater mode**:
Turn off your screen
and silence incoming
calls and notifications.

- **Do Not Disturb**:
Silence all incoming
calls and disable all
notifications. To
configure exceptions
for priority and repeat
callers, alerts, and
media sounds, press
and hold.

- **Battery Saver**:
Disable Always-On
Display and Tilt-to-
Wake.

- **Touch lock**:
Disable touch
interaction on the
display.

- **🌙Bedtime mode**: Turn off all notifications with the exception of alarms, priority, and repeat calls.

Chapter 7: Phone calls and SMS texts on Google Pixel Watch

Google Pixel Watch allows users to make phone calls and send text messages. You can authorize access to your phone's contact list during setup by managing the associated Google Account on file.

You can modify the Google Account associated with your watch at any time:

- Swipe down on the Google Pixel Watch and then tap Settings.
- Review Accounts and security.
- Connect or disconnect a Google Account to your watch.

Requirements

- mobile phone cellular service
- Cellular service for the Google Pixel Watch LTE.

Phone calls

Google Pixel Watch LTE: Verify that you have a cellular watch

1. On Google Pixel Watch, swipe down

and then tap Settings

.

2. Tap Connectivity and
    then Mobile.

If you don't see a Mobile
setting, your watch does not
support cellular service. You
must have Google Pixel
Watch LTE to get cellular
service on your watch. You
must use the same carrier for
watch and phone service.

**Google Pixel Watch Wi-Fi:
Verify that you are
connected to Bluetooth
and Wi-Fi**

1. On Google Pixel
    Watch, swipe down
    and then tap Settings

    .

2. Tap Connectivity and
    then Bluetooth and

then turn on
Bluetooth.

3. Swipe right to go back
    a menu and tap Wi-Fi
    and then turn on Wi-
    Fi.

Place or answer a call

Make and receive calls with
Google Pixel Watch using the
built-in microphone and
speaker or Bluetooth-
connected headphones.

Note: A nearby phone is not
required to make or receive a
call with Google Pixel Watch
LTE.

Ask Google Assistant to make
and answer a call or by
tapping a contact's name
from your watch:

1. On Google Pixel
    Watch, press the side

button next to the
crown.

2. Scroll down and then
   tap Contacts.

3. Select or search for a
   contact name.

4. Tap the chosen
   contact name.

5. To place a call, tap the
   phone next to their
   number .

Text and SMS

With the Android messaging
app set as the default
messaging client on your
phone, you can send and
receive text and SMS
messages on Google Pixel
Watch.

Note: Google Pixel Watch
syncs texts with your phone
so your connected phone
must be online.

**Type and send a Text or
SMS message**

Answer a message or by
tapping a contact's name
from your watch.

1. To use the Google
   Pixel Watch, press the
   crown.

2. Scroll down and then
   tap Contacts.

3. Select or search for a
   contact name.

4. Tap the chosen
   contact name.

5. To draft a message,
   tap the message box
   next to their number
   .

You can also ask Google
Assistant to send a text or
read and reply with swipe
actions.

Chapter 8: Wear and adjust Google Pixel Watch

Adjust the size of the band on your Google Pixel Watch for comfort, and change the band to match your personal style.

Connect a band

1. Flip over your Google Pixel Watch.
2. Utilize the band to depress the band release button, then slide the band into position.
3. Continue on the reverse side.

Remove a band

1. Flip over your Google Pixel Watch.
2. Press the band release button, then slip the band over the band and release the button as you draw the band away from the watch.
3. Continue on the reverse side.

Wear the Google Pixel Watch

For the Active band (included with Google Pixel Watch). The application instructions for other bands will differ.

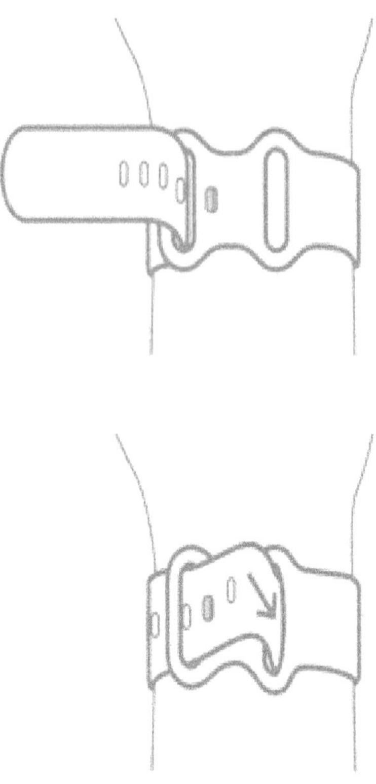

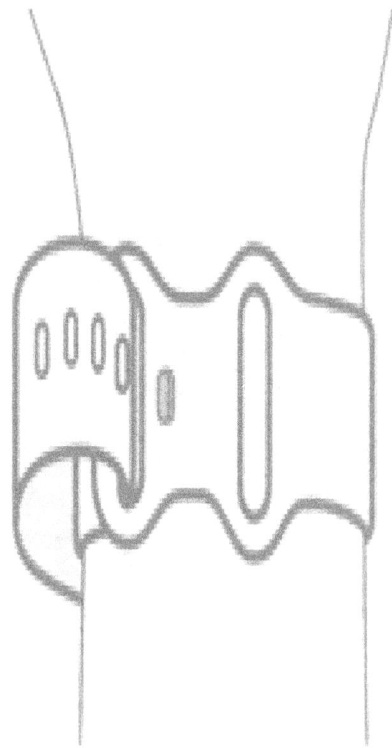

Take off Google Pixel Watch

1. Pull the strap through the outer loop.
2. Insert the metal rod into the hole.
3. Tuck the band in. If it is excessively long, try the tiny band.

1. Remove the band.
2. To release the peg, you must flex the band backwards.

Wrist orientation

Choose wrist orientation according to the hand on which you wear your watch.

Regarding Google Pixel Watch

1. Tap Settings on the Google Pixel Watch, then tap About. Manifest and then Wrist inclination

2. Choose the wrist on which you will wear your watch.

3. Scroll down and select the crown's position.

4. Tap the checkbox and scroll down to save your settings.

The Google Pixel Watch application

1. On your mobile device, launch the Google Pixel Watch

    app .

2. Select Watch preferences, followed by Watch orientation.

3. Choose which wrist the watch is worn on and where the crown is located.

Chapter 9: Google Assistant voice commands on Google Pixel Watch

Set up Google Assistant

Google Pixel Watch is equipped with Google Assistant for alarms, messages, and useful information.

1. Tap and hold the side button next to the crown on the Pixel Watch .

2. To activate, touch Get started and then Open on phone.

3. On your mobile device, launch the Google Pixel Watch app.

4. Tap Setup followed by Activate.

5. Examine the various features that can be enabled or disabled.

6. Configure your Hey Google or Ok Google trigger phrase.

    a. If you haven't previously, use Voice Match to train the voice model.

Use Google Assistant

There are multiple ways to enable Google Assistant on the Google Pixel Watch.

- Side button: Tap and hold the side button adjacent to the crown on the Google Pixel Watch.
- Say "Hey, Google" or "Okay, Google." The Google Pixel Watch must be awake in order to listen for your passphrase. You may wake your watch by touching on the display, hitting any button, or using the tilt-to-wake feature.
- Tap Assistant on your watch face if you've installed Assistant Assistant as a complication.

Examples of what you can ask

To elicit suggestions, ask "What can you do?" Your Assistant can assist you with:

Keep in touch

- Dial: Dial Davey.
- Messages: Send Layla a message.

Manage your plans

- When is my next scheduled meeting?
- Alarms: Set a 7 a.m. alarm.

Get directions and answers

- Find the closest coffee shop by navigation.
- What will the weather be like tomorrow?

Control music

- Play my exercise playlist, please.
- Volume: Volume up.

Maintain Google Home

- Please turn off my lights.
- Lock my front door, please.

Track fitness

- Exercise: Start a run.

Control smart home devices

Google Pixel Watch enables Google Assistant management of smart home devices such as lighting and thermostats.

Google Assistant is capable of controlling smart home gadgets.

Disable hotword

1. Google Assistant must be activated on the Google Pixel Watch.
2. Wait for the "Hello, how may I assist you?" or "Go ahead, I'm listening" windows to transition to "Try saying."
3. Swipe up on the display and select Settings.
4. Toggle "Hey Google" off.

Google Assistant and your privacy

- If you are unable to connect to Google Assistant or send messages on your Google Pixel Watch, try the steps in Fix difficulties with

Google Assistant on
your watch.

- Google Assistant and
  confidentiality
- Check out the Google
  Assistant Safety
  Center.
- Select which
  information to share
  with Google Assistant.
- Your voice and audio
  data are kept
  confidential while
  Google Assistant is
  enhanced.
- Check out the Google
  Assistant Safety
  Center.

Chapter 10: Charge Google Pixel Watch and improve battery life

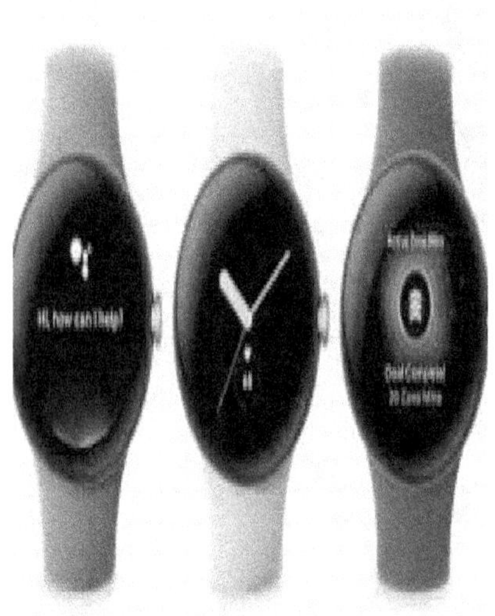

With a charge that lasts up to 24 hours, the battery life of the Google Pixel Watch is sufficient to support sleep monitoring and other capabilities throughout the day. Google Pixel Watch includes settings for battery maintenance and life extension.

Charge Google Pixel Watch

1. Connect the accompanying Google Pixel Watch USB-C Magnetic Charging Cable to an electrical outlet.
2. Place the watch on the magnetic charging cable's end.
3. The Google Pixel Watch screen will wake up and display the percentage of charge, date, and time to signal that the device is charging. It takes approximately 30 minutes to reach 50% charge, 55 minutes to reach 80%,

and 80 minutes to reach 100%. One watch will not charge

Watch won't charge

- If the Google Pixel Watch has not been charging, the issue could be a faulty charger connection.
  - After several seconds of an erroneous charger connection, a notification should appear on the watch. Remove and replace the watch in order to resolve this issue.
- Using an incompatible charger or charging station, such as a wireless charging pad, with a Pixel phone.
  - Reverse wireless charging is not supported for Pixel smartphones.
  - Google Pixel Watch can only be charged with the magnetic charging cable included with the device. Utilizing it will resolve the issue.

Extend battery life

Battery Defender

If your Google Pixel Watch is charged for four days or

more, Battery Defender will suspend charging to protect the battery. If the battery level of your Google Pixel Watch remains below 80%, you may have Battery Defender on. When activated, a notification should appear when awakening or removing the Google Pixel Watch from its charger. To continue charging the watch over 80%, remove it from the charger and then replace it.

Improve battery life

These strategies can help extend the battery life of your Google Pixel Watch.

Battery Saver

Battery Saver can be activated when the Pixel Watch's battery is low.

While Battery Saver is enabled, "Always-on screen" and "Tilt-to-wake" will be disabled.

1. Swipe down on the Google Pixel Watch and then tap Settings ⚙.

2. Tap Battery .
3. Enable "Battery saver"
4. Tap OK.

Full Doze Mode

Not available on the Google Pixel Watch LTE with an active Verizon plan.

Full Doze Mode Is a power-saving function that switches off the Google Pixel Watch screen and all modem radios (LTE, Wi-Fi, Bluetooth) after 10 minutes of inactivity when the device is not being worn, charged, or used. When you wear your watch on your wrist or when you interact with it, Full Doze Mode will be disabled.

- Find My Device will not update the location of devices in Full Doze Mode.
- When Full Doze Mode is on, using the watch, such as during a phone call, pauses the doze timer.
- Your watch will lack network connectivity, and all radios will be disabled.

Always-on screen

Always-on screen keeps your watch's display from turning black even when you are not using it. To increase the battery life of your watch, you can disable this feature.

The Always-on screen feature will be disabled by default on your watch.

1. Swipe down on the Google Pixel Watch and then tap Settings ⚙.

2. Tap Display, then deactivate "Always-on screen."

Tilt-to-wake

Google Pixel Watch's Tilt-to-wake feature activates the display when the device is tilted. To increase the battery life of your watch, you can disable this feature.

Your watch will arrive with the Tilt-to-wake feature disabled.

1. Swipe down on the Google Pixel Watch and then tap Settings .

2. Tap Gestures, then disable "Tilt-to-wake."

Bedtime mode

Enable Bedtime mode for less battery consumption and fewer interruptions overnight when using the watch to track sleep.

GPS

Enable Google Location Precision for the most energy-efficient location data.

1. Swipe down on the Google Pixel Watch and then tap Settings.

2. Tap Location, then Google Location Accuracy, and then toggle Improve location accuracy to the on position.

Note that the battery life of the Google Pixel Watch is 8 to 10 hours with constant GPS use.

Mobile Mode (LTE only)

Activating the watch's eSIM enables cellular radio connectivity on the Google Pixel Watch LTE. If your Google Pixel Watch loses power too quickly when connected to a network, you can extend its battery life by configuring Mobile Mode to Automatic or Off.

Automatically connect to cellular radio only when Bluetooth or Wi-Fi connectivity is unavailable.

Off: Completely deactivate the mobile radio.

1. Swipe down on the Google Pixel Watch and then tap Settings ⚙.
2. Tap Connectivity followed by Mobile and Mobile.
3. Select Auto or Off.

When your phone is offline and Mobile is Off, you will be unable to access certain capabilities, such as making phone calls.

Download music

Streaming music might deplete batteries faster than downloading music.

Change screen timeout settings

Change the rate at which your watch face goes to sleep to conserve power.

1. Swipe down on your Google Pixel Watch and then tap Settings ⚙.
2. Tap Display, then Display timeout.
3. Choose a shorter timeout.

Chapter 11: Activity and sleep tracking on Google Pixel Watch

Fitbit's all-day activity and heart-rate tracking, sleep tracking, and other features will assist you in achieving your health and fitness objectives.

Note: You must log in to a Fitbit account through the Google Pixel Watch app in order to track historical activity and sleep statistics.

Connect your Fitbit account

Connect your Fitbit account at any moment or during setup.

1. To use the Google Pixel Watch, press the crown.

2. Tap Fitbit Today followed by Login.

3. On your mobile device, log in. If the Fitbit app is not installed on your phone, tap Install, then Open, and then Join Fitbit. Then, follow the steps displayed on-screen to create a Fitbit account.

4. First-time Fitbit users:
   Select the Google Pixel
   Watch from the
   selection of watches
   during Fitbit account
   creation.

Current Fitbit users: Add the
Google Pixel Watch to your
Fitbit profile by navigating to
your account profile in the
upper-left corner of the Fitbit
app's home page, and then
selecting Set Up a Device.

5. When prompted,
   configure the app's
   permissions.

Heart-rate tracking and ECG

Google Pixel Watch can
monitor your heart rate
throughout the day and
provide workout-specific
data such as Active Zone
Minutes.

The Fitbit ECG app1 loaded
from the Google Play Store
for Google Pixel Watch can
monitor your heart rhythm.
Your cardiac rhythm data is
evaluated for indications of
AFib when you use the Fitbit
ECG app. Although only a
physician can diagnose AFib,
the findings of this
evaluation can assist
determine whether your
heart rhythm exhibits
indications of the disorder.
Learn more about the Fitbit
ECG app's qualifying
conditions by visiting
Irregular rhythm.

Heart-rate tracking and ECG

Set sleep objectives, monitor sleep stages, and manage reminders to unwind. For sleep tracking, your device must have at least a 30% charge (about 30 minutes to 50%). Consider charging during your morning routine or before bed so that the battery will survive while you sleep.

Track exercise, fitness, and activity goals

Google Pixel Watch automatically tracks multiple types of activities. Google Pixel Watch can track steps, calories, GPS data, and more for activities such as running, weightlifting, and tennis.

Activate Fitbit Premium features

Fitbit Premium's 6-month trial is included with every Google Pixel Watch purchase.

1. Sign in to your Fitbit account via Google Pixel Watch.
2. On your phone, open Fitbit .
3. Tap Premium.
4. Follow the steps on-screen to redeem the trial.